Restore

The Pastor's

Authority!

Only Pastors Are Elders!

Who's in Charge?

Boards, Apostles and Deacons

Restore

The Pastor's

Authority!

Only Pastors Are Elders!

Who's in Charge?

Boards, Apostles and Deacons

Harry Ramey

Old Mountain Press

Reader's note:
All quotations found in this work from the Bible are from the NIV.

Published by:
Old Mountain Press, Inc.
2542 S. Edgewater Dr.
Fayetteville, NC 28303

www.oldmountainpress.com

ISBN: 1-931575-27-4
Library of Congress Control Number: 2003103595

Restore the Pastor's Authority!: Only Pastors are elders! Who's in Charge? Boards, Apostles and Deacons.

First Edition
Printed and bound in the United States of America by Morris Publishing •
www.morrispublishing.com • 800-650-7888
1 2 3 4 5 6 7 8 9 10

CONTENTS

INTRODUCTION

While pastoring in Missouri about five weeks into a new building, I experienced a church split–which is as close to hell as you can get on a pew. The dispute revolved around the question, What are elders? When I finally got my head above the smoke, I saw elder board brush fires burning in other Charismatic churches in my area.

Another question that lay beneath the rumbling was, Who's in charge? Now, 22 years later, I find these same questions still being asked. So I took my research paper that I did when my burns were fresh and expanded it into this book. You may not agree with my findings. But at least my conclusions will prime your pump for your own study.

I believe the pastor's in charge; I'm in your face with that fact. But I also take a couple of chapters to balance that position. Approach this study with an open mind whether you're a pastor or a lay-elder. (There's no such thing.)

CHAPTER 1

THE CHARISMATIC ELDER BOARD

In the 80's, fledgling Charismatic churches, in their haste to be scriptural, rushed to select elders from the congregation: Select elders first, and find out what they are later.

These elders were usually solid, good-brother types, who could get along with a live-in mother-in-law going through menopause.

Various means were used to choose elders. Just being old (elderly) helped in places; some churches would "elderize" all department heads to constitute a board; and some desperate congregations might tap you as an elder as you rise from the altar, wet-eyed from conversion. If you're a successful businessman, you may be elder material. Just look "elderish" in an off moment and you may get the call.

In other words, the elder profile differed from church to church.

THE GOOD-BROTHEROCRACY

The good-brotherocracy runs smoothly for a time, though getting a decision through one of these boards sometimes is like crossing the L.A. freeway in a wheelchair!

Eventually, trouble develops. Several brothers disagree with the way the pastor is doing things. (Why didn't he consult us? We wanted Puffs in the ladies' restroom, not Kleenex.)

Soon it's easy for several elders to call a special prayer meeting on the side without the pastor. (We're concerned about *our* church.)

A confrontation may ensue: Pastor, we've decided it would be in your best interests to leave (since you won't let us deliver you from that spirit of domination).

The *H* word may be aired about this time: Remember, we hired you! The word *hire* betrays an underlying assumption: the good brothers now regard the pastor as their employee. And if you can hire him, you can fire him! You now have a *hireling* instead of a shepherd.

The old, traditional church board spirit has now possessed the elders!

This doesn't happen in every case. Sometimes men of excellent disposition land in board seats. But it happens often. I knew of a group of Charismatic churches strung along an interstate in the Midwest, and all of them suffered from some degree of "elderitus."

TEMPORARY ELDERS

In my new church in Missouri, I tried calling my board *temporary* elders. I wanted time to see who was a real elder. But my temporary elders declared themselves *permanent.* Then they decided I was temporary (a *temporary* problem).

When you call some men *temporary* elders, they don't hear the word *temporary.* Once some guys become elders, they consider it a life appointment, like a federal judge!

A highly respected minister figure was brought in to mediate my elder situation. There was no temporary solution with my temporary elders. It wound up splitting the church. This train-wreck experience with elders set me to researching. I wanted to know what elders really are, what hoops a man must jump through to be an elder, and how high to set the bar.

We Charismatics thought we had shucked the old traditional church government. I found we had only traded hubcaps and kept the car. My research surprised me. I sneaked up on myself! My conclusions may surprise you.

I found there's very little difference between the Charismatic elder board and the traditional Baptist deacon board. What's disturbing to me now is that more churches are going to lay, elder-type government. A *council* member of a local church here told me the other day that the council could sell the church without even the pastor's consent! This is an ongoing trend in Pentecostal and Charismatic churches. In this book, I take issue with that trend. It's unscriptural.

CHAPTER 2

ONLY PASTORS ARE ELDERS

The root of the *elder* problem is a misunderstanding of what elders really are. (Will the real elders please stand up?)

I'm going to make a statement: *Only pastors are elders.* In case that didn't hit at least a 5 on your doctrinal Richter scale, let me run that by you again. I didn't say that elders should do pastoral things, such as visiting the hospital or making the announcements on Sunday morning. I said *only* pastors are elders!

A pastor looking for a true elder needs only look in the mirror–or only look at the assistant pastors under him.

Believers who are not pastors are not elders. If you are not anointed, appointed, gifted, called, functioning as a pastor, or able to function as a pastor, you are not an elder. If you can't fill a pastor's office, you can't fill an elder's office. There is no such creature as a *lay-elder*!

Once this fact is understood, a lot of fog lifts. (Never buy better fog lights if you can get rid of the fog!)

SHEEP AND SHEPHERDS

In a congregation, there are sheep and shepherds. Sheep are not shepherds. Even super sheep are not shepherds (even those on steroids). Putting a shepherd's mantle on a sheep and having him meet with the shepherd once a week doesn't make him a shepherd.

Natural (dumb?) sheep have no trouble knowing they're not the shepherd. The strongest sheep would never consider himself co-equal with the shepherd (or try to *ram* anything through).

God has placed a microcosm of his government within these wooly parallels of his people. It's government by shepherds not government by sheep (*shepherdocracy*)!

The church has stepped outside this basic knowledge and put sheep (believers who are not shepherds) in the office of shepherds, co-pastoring the church (*sheepocracy*). The Charismatic lay-elder board expresses this error as much as the Baptist deacon board does. Presbyterians, whose very name is taken from the Greek word for elder, *presbuteros,* miss this point also!

When a lay-elder board meets with the pastor, only one elder is present–the pastor!

SHEPHERDS RULE SHEEP!

But you, Bethlehem, in the land of Judah, are by no means least among the rulers of Judah; for out of you will come a ruler who will be shepherd of my people Israel. (Matt. 2:6)

I will place over them one shepherd, my servant David, and he will tend them; he will tend them and be their shepherd. (Ez. 34:23)

Now the overseer must be above reproach....he must manage his own family well....If anyone does not know how to manage his own family, how can he take care of God's church? (1Tim. 3:2a, 4a, 5)

The local overseer, the pastor, is supposed to *manage* his family well. *Manage* is *proestimi* in Greek. It means "to rule, to have authority over." The pastor is to rule, have authority over, manage the church like he manages his own family! (Unless, of course, the pastor's family is a disaster!)

The very term *overseer* implies authority. It is a translation of *episkopos*–to have oversight. Picture a foreman on the job; he's an *episkopos* because he directs and oversees the work!

Church members who would never think of the pastor as being head over the local church work under some kind of foreman every day. Very few employers operate their company as a democracy! Where I currently work, my boss may elicit input from us, but we're under no delusions as to who's in charge!

Sure, the pastor of the local church doesn't rule with the same rigidity as your boss. But he should be recognized as being in charge.

Shepherds rule sheep! That statement would send a ripple of laughter down a row of seminary professors. Such *radical* thinking has been buried under this culture's intellectual scorn. But it was God who chose to call the leader of his church a *poimen* (Greek for *shepherd* or *pastor*).

For shepherds to rule sheep is not a new idea. What's new and unscriptural is for a committee of sheep to rule over the shepherd (a big sheep oligarchy)!

When sheep oversee the shepherd, the shepherd's authority is diluted. He is like a policeman who must get permission from the town council before he can issue a ticket (especially if it's a councilman's son who's being arrested). The pastor's authority to reprove and correct is now subject to the sheep's input and approval. It's like letting kids in class vote before a teacher can correct. (School has almost come to that.)

In some cases, the shepherd winds up with a symbolic rod which ends up in the devil's closet after it's traded for a backscratcher! The pastor is reduced to a surgeon with a rubber scalpel; he can tickle you but can't cut to the problem. The pastor's authority in places is like English kings and queens who are only royal relics, living traditions, with the real authority resting in parliament!

Under such conditions, many pastors decide to exercise their authority anyway, but it's better to live in a mobile home instead of a parsonage if they do. Co-equal boards, lay-elders, deacon boards, and oversight committees can tie a pastor's hands behind his back. An imposing board member with big bucks in his back pocket can hint to a pastor discreetly that a certain kind of preaching *may not be in the pastor's best interest.*

A board exercises an even greater tidal pull on a pastor when it controls his salary: Purse strings can be puppet strings. To say "The pastor can see to the spiritual interests of the church, but we'll take care of the finances" sounds good, but many a pastor has found out too late that checks and balances means that whoever writes the checks can decide if the pastor's balanced! Since elders direct the affairs of the church (1 Tim. 5:17), the pastor should be involved in or direct any major financial decisions. Some pastors, out of humility, decide to let advisors recommend the pastor's pay raises. That works in many situations.

The pastor must have scriptural authority to take care of the church as he rules his own house (1Tim. 3:2). Am I saying a pastor should rule as a monarch? Nonsense! In another chapter I'll explain how the pastor obtains balance in that position.

One more thing. Certainly apostles are elders too (1 Peter 5:2). After all, apostles pastor pastors!

Pastor has the right to have a say in Pastoral Pay Package.

CHAPTER 3

NECKSHIP

A shepherd is not accountable to the sheep for his performance! I know, falling on American ears, that's heresy (Harrysey).

But when you make the shepherd accountable to the sheep, the sheep are the final authority. And when sheep have the final say, they'll finally say it!

When the sheep are in charge, a figurehead leader will usually emerge from this arrangement— that is, the pastor is the *head* as long as the board *figures* it's best! An elder or deacon can sometimes negate the pastor's authority with his vote.

This is *giraffe* government–*neckship*–a big strong neck with a small head.

Once the pastor's authority is compromised, it's hard to fearlessly, faithfully correct and train with the Word, knowing that the toes you step on may belong to the feet that can kick you out. The final opinion rests with those you govern. (Rejection at election time is hard on family finances.)

Of course, pastors under any system will be under pressure to appease, please, and try to avoid the squeeze put on by dollar situations. It's unnerving while you're preaching to see a frown spread across the face of someone that represents a tenth of your church budget. But while the truth should be spoken in love (Eph. 4:15), a good pastor knows that everyone won't love the truth. There'll always be opportunities to do right and ignore the consequences.

A HEAD OVER THE HEAD!

A pastor should be accountable to a head over him. An apostle or regional overseer should examine the pastor if charges are brought against him (1 Tim. 5:17-20). Where no apostle is present, a pastor might submit himself to a presbytery, a group of pastors, if this option is workable. A clear understanding should be had beforehand of the limits of this arrangement.

Who?

In 1 Timothy 5:17-23, the apostle (Timothy in Paul's place here) clearly had authority over pastors. He could hear charges against them, rebuke them for sinning, and decide if and when to ordain them! (We need to rediscover apostles; although the term has "dinosaured," the office is still with us.)

Scripturally, pastors were appointed (Titus 1:5). They were not rounded up by a nomination committee, voted in, voted out, elected, or rejected by some political process. In some places the *goat* vote rules the process. To get into some churches, a pastor must win some faction's beauty contest! Church politics makes Democrats and Republicans look like political pussycats. However, once congregational rule is established, people usually won't give it up. The solution is sometimes to start over.

Every *undershepherd*, pastor, is accountable to the Chief Shepherd (1 Peter 5:4). But most boards think there should be some controlling human limits on the pastor besides God–after all, God doesn't vote! (See the chapter "When the Pastor Gets Weird.")

While a shepherd doesn't give account to the sheep as to his performance, financial disclosure is always in order. Paul was very careful not only to do right, but also to give not even the appearance of doing wrong, especially with money (2 Cor. 8). Church money should always be seen with several sets of eyes. *Who?*

HOW LAY-ELDERS SEE THINGS

A pastor is obligated to get direction from God. But, often, lay-elders–who have just pulled their heads out of a secular business meeting–will bring a pie-chart mentality into the church board meeting. Don't misunderstand; we should be business-like with God's business. But sometimes God can't be charted and graphed!

The Holy Spirit may say, "Build debt free." However, your *Quicken* software may rupture itself trying to graph that idea with the church's income. Just remember: God's not tethered to the board's calculator.

To a secular-minded board member, whose prayer life consists of grace said at power lunches, a pastor's vision can look like secular suicide. This is not to say that all lay-elders are secular minded. Some of the most spiritual men I've known have been non-pastors (and some of the pastors I've known would have flunked spiritual Romper Room). Titles don't always match positions. But you get my drift: to give totally secular people equal vote with a God-seeking pastor on a board is to invite complete gridlock.

Give the pastor room to hear God. Support him in prayer! Allow him to make some mistakes. Let God's man be God's man!

CHAPTER 4

THINGS FINALLY COME TO A *HEAD!*

Most of life's situations require someone to be in charge. A ship doesn't steer well with a dozen co-equal captains in the pilothouse, as many hands on the wheel, and everyone listening to his own wireless. E v e n worldly sense begs someone to be in charge. A movie has a director, a ship has a captain, an army has a general, a class has a teacher, and an airliner with only two pilots names one of them as captain! An octopus has eight arms but only one head. (God save us from a schizophrenic octopus!) The allies in World War II saw the need for one commander over all the European armies–Eisenhower.

A little-league coach has latitude in making decisions that most pastors only dream of. Play the following scenario in your mind: it's two out in the ninth; who'll pinch-hit? Shall the parents in the stands vote? Shall the players (sheep) form a committee with the coach (lay-play-elders)? The coach (pastor) may consult with the assistants (plurality) and may get input from the parents (count on it in little leagues), but the final decision is the coach's!

Some churches have as much trouble coming to a decision as Siamese twins having two-o'clock tickets to different movies! I'm not talking about waiting on God; sometimes that's necessary and takes a while. I'm talking about unwieldy church governments that can't decide who should decide what should be decided.

HEADSHIP ABOUNDS

A church should have a clear head. Why should that be such a camel to swallow? Feminists will draw up their toes, but I'll say it anyway: *Even a family of two has a head* (1 Cor. 11:3). Sorry, I don't have time to get into what kind of head the man should be, a Christ-like, gentle, servant, lay-down-your-life-for-your-wife head, but a head nonetheless!

Even the Godhead, with three perfect divine persons, has a head!

Now I want you to realize that the head of every man is Christ, and the head of the woman is the man, and the head of Christ is God. (1 Cor. 11:3)

For he "has put everything under his feet." Now when it says that "everything" has been put under him, it is clear that this does not include God himself, who put everything under Christ.

When he has done this, then the Son himself will be subject to him who

Put everything under him, so that God may be all in all. (1 Cor. 15:27, 28)

So the Son himself will be under his head, the Father, when we come to the eternal age. If Christ considers it no disgrace to submit to a head, why should we? Should we be part of the rebellion that characterizes this age and will usher in a time like Sodom?

The Old Testament is not short on heads either.

May the Lord appoint a man over the congregation, who will go out and come in before them...that the congregation of the Lord may not be like sheep which have no shepherd.

So the Lord said..."Take Joshua...and lay your hands on him." (Num. 27:16-18)

Among Israel's elders (pastor-like leaders of tribes), Moses was head. Call him senior pastor, super shepherd, prime presbyter, head honcho, or whatever. He's the elder, bishop, shepherd; he's God's man. God speaks to him and through him. He is not always right, but it's never right to rebel against him. (Ask Miriam and Aaron–Numbers 12.)

The charisma to lead will rest on a man among God's people. Look at any local congregation, he'll stand out! He is the shepherd; he may have assistants under him, but he is the head. He is the principal shepherd.

The pastor, as the head, gathers, guards, and guides. He is anointed to see that sheep are led, fed, and don't turn up dead and produce others in their stead.

CO-EQUAL PASTORS

Where there is more than one pastor, one should be the head, the senior pastor. Co-equal pastors work on rare occasions. Sometimes a strong-willed pastor meshes with a weak-willed pastor and it appears to be co-equal. Put two strong-willed pastors together, and it will eventually evolve into two congregations. Better to have a clear head to start with!

BOSSY PROPHETS

Prophets are listed before pastors in Ephesians 4:11. Does that mean the pastor is under the local prophets? A prophetess in my congregation took me to task because the church wasn't doing all God was telling her it should do. In other words, she wanted to control the church through prophecy. I *enlightened* her: I let her know there were other churches in the yellow pages that could use her services.

Prophets who want to control churches are *pew witches.* They're listening to another spirit! Prophets should be respected and listened to, but under the New Covenant where we all have the Holy Spirit, prophecy should confirm, not direct. No prophet, by virtue of his office, is over the pastor.

And who says the Bible always lists things in the order of their importance? Love is listed last in 1 Corinthians 13:13, yet it's the greatest.

IS IT DANGEROUS TO HAVE ONE MAN AS HEAD?

Isn't it dangerous to call a man the head (under Christ) of the church? Are we setting up a situation that may morph a Jim Jones? Are we creating a Catholic-type hierarchy?

Why don't we have the same fear about cliques gaining control of the church? Or factions? Or boards that evolve into oligarchies, excluding others? Or churches that fall under the control of a prominent family? Why not apply the Jim Jones fear to those situations? A collective Jim Jones is no better than an individual Jim Jones!

People sometimes use the Jim Jones fear as an excuse to retain power themselves. The apostles were definite heads over their areas with no apologies (1 Tim. 5:17-22). And the Greek terms in the New Testament lend themselves to headship.

A FIVE-FOLD MINISTRY IN EVERY CHURCH?

Some say that every local church should have all five ministry offices in it: apostle, prophet, evangelist, pastor, and teacher (Eph. 4:11, 12).

Why? Where is the scriptural requirement for that? An apostle is over groups of churches in an area. Why would an apostle be needed in every local church?

For a church to be spiritually accredited, must it have a resident apostle? Must the five-fold ministries be present to have a quorum? If the local prophet is a no-show today (He watched the playoffs!) do we call off the service? And what about the other gift ministries? Is the ministry of healing required to be there? And what about the tongues-speaker? And the interpreter? Do we need all the spiritual gifts present to function? (1 Cor. 12:28-30)

Give me a break! Remember, Paul addressed his Philippian letter to the *overseers and deacons* of Philippi. There was no apostle in every local Philippian church. After all, Paul was their apostle! To start with, every local church needs a pastor. Visiting ministries are welcome, but the pastor's in charge under the apostle!

THE FLOATING HEADSHIP

Some Charismatic elder boards in the 80's courted the idea of a *floating headship*. That is, the anointing to head the church would rest on one brother for a while then another (a lousy way to get a *head*).

Talk about confusion! Wait till two brothers both claim the headship.

By what criteria do we recognize the headship anointing? Who's anointed to determine who's anointed? Don't think flesh won't seize the opportunity for headship under a butterfly anointing system. (When the headship floats, the church may sink!)

You don't glide in and out of the office of pastor (musical chairs ministry). The office doesn't have a revolving door. Even a natural flock of sheep won't jive with rotating shepherds. Imagine soldiers going into battle not knowing who's *generaling* that day (*general* nonsense).

No church gets ahead without getting a *head*!

HEADSTRONG!

Sometimes department leaders get the idea that they are heads over their corners of the church: the worship leader has sovereignty over the worship; the youth leader is the sole leader of youth, and so on. The pastor is just another head among the heads. He has his areas to oversee.

No ship would operate like that. Imagine the galley chief telling the captain to bug out of the kitchen, or the officer on the bridge deciding on his own to change the course of the ship. You don't have five independent captains running their respective departments. The same is true in church. All department heads are under the pastor. The only thing worse than having no head is having too many!

Security rests with established headship. Let the shepherd *shep* and head things up and not be sheepish about it.

CHAPTER 5

PASTOR, ELDER, BISHOP, OR YOU CAN CALL ME....

D id the Greeks use several different words for the office of pastor? Were these words used interchangeably? Were pastors sometimes called elders? Or bishops?

In Acts 20, Paul calls for the elders of the church at Ephesus:

> From Miletus, Paul sent to Ephesus for the elders of the church. (vs. 17)

Watch carefully: these same elders are called *overseers* in verse 28:

> Keep watch over yourselves and all the flock of which the Holy Spirit has made you overseers....

Plainly, elders and overseers here are the same people–the same office!

Now some translate the Greek word for overseer as *bishop.* So elders and overseers/bishops are the same persons. Paul uses these terms interchangeably in Titus 1.

The reason I left you in Crete was that you might straighten out what was left unfinished and appoint <u>elders</u> in every town as I directed you. (vs. 5)

In verse 7 Paul calls these elders *overseers*:

…since an overseer is entrusted with God's work....

But we're not through with passages in Acts 20. These same men are called something else:

Be <u>shepherds</u> of the church of God, which he bought with his own blood....(vs. 28)

So, the same men are called elders, overseers/bishops, and shepherds!

A SHEPHERD IS A PASTOR!

We've worn the term *pastor* smooth. We almost forgotten it means *shepherd*!

By his very position, the pastor is elder (prominent leader) and overseer of the flock. No wonder these terms are interchangeable.

WHERE ARE THE EPHESIAN ELDERS?

Paul called for the elders of the church of Ephesus to meet him in Acts 20. He writes to the same Ephesians about church leaders in Ephesians 4.

It was he (Christ) who gave some to be apostles, some to be prophets,
Some to be evangelists, and some to be pastors and teachers. (vs. 11)

Notice, Paul does not mention elders! Yet he had called for the elders of this church to meet him in Acts 20! How can the apostle talk about leaders to this church and not mention elders?

Simple. What Paul calls *elders* in Acts 20, he calls *pastors* in Ephesians 4! To Paul, pastors and elders are the same.

Again, the office of shepherd, by its very nature, includes being elder and overseer of the flock.

If elders were laymen, would Paul have called for lay-elders in Acts 20 and not for the pastors? Unthinkable. Would James have called for the elders of the church to pray for the sick and not called for the pastors (James 5:14)? The elders of the church are the pastors (probably one senior pastor and assistants, or several city pastors close by).

When the pastor is called *elder* it references his maturity and leadership.

Paul could have called the leaders of the Ephesus church *overseers.*

To all the saints in Christ Jesus at Philippi, together with the overseers and deacons. (Phil. 1:1b)

Three terms are used for the same office in 1 Peter 5:

To the <u>elders</u> among you, I appeal as a fellow elder.... be <u>shepherds</u> (<u>pastors</u>) of God's flock that is under your care, serving as <u>overseers</u>....(vss. 1a, 2a)

Plainly, these terms are used interchangeably.

In 1 Peter 2:25, Jesus is Shepherd (pastor) and overseer (bishop) of our souls (the same office).

Call the man who heads up the local church *shepherd, pastor, overseer, bishop, elder,* or you can call him *Ray or you can call him Jay....* Hey! It's the same office!

CHAPTER 6

IT'S GREEK TO ME!

The New Testament was written in Greek. Greek is *Greek* to most people these days, but in the first century it was spoken worldwide. (The last Greek I heard was over a gyro.)

Any in-depth New Testament word study begs a peek at the Greek. I'm not a Greek geek, but Greek word studies are now available to Joe Average. You can mouse up to the tool bar and pull down good Greek heads all day long, or pull a commentary off the shelf and sift through dead men's brains for good Greek stuff.

Let's look at some Greek terms that are commonly used instead of *pastor.*

ELDER

The Greek word for *elder* is *presbuteros.* This Greek word saddlebags several meanings. It can mean an old man. (I am now an "elder" in this sense. Luke 15:25; John 8:9) It can mean *ancestors* or the *ancients* (Mark 7:3, 5; Heb. 11:2). It can refer to prominent leaders, regardless of age (1 Tim. 4:12).

Presbuteros usually specifies an official leader. To Jews, elders were tribal leaders, members of the Sanhedrin, and so on. The phrase *chief priests and elders* pops up often in the New Testament. When the context doesn't call for *old men*, the *presbuteroi* are the prominent leaders.

LOCAL CHURCH ELDERS

The reason I left you in Crete (Paul to Titus) was that you might straighten out what was left unfinished and appoint elders in every town as I directed you. (Titus 1:5)

What were these elders that Titus appointed? Lay oversight committees? Lay-elders? Ask yourself: would Paul have appointed lay-elders in every city without appointing pastors? The elders here are pastors.

In Acts 14:21-23, Paul and Barnabas appoint elders in every church. Would Paul, with his vast knowledge, appoint laymen over churches leaving them without shepherds?

Or did Paul appoint pastors and key laymen as elders in the churches? Are pastors simply one of the elders? Many Charismatic churches have combo boards made up of pastors and laymen. Look carefully; you never see the phrase *the pastor and the elders* in Scripture.

Look at a flock of sheep with a shepherd standing over them. Who is the *presbuteros*? The elder? (If you picked the fattest sheep, retake the test!) The shepherd is the elder, the *presbuteros*, the *episkopos*, the overseer, the bishop, the pastor!

Presbuteros can also be translated *presbyter*. (If you're looking for a name for a denomination, though, *Presbyterian* is taken!)

A group of pastors or pastors and apostles over an area would be called a *presbytery*. This group of elders would come together to ordain ministers (usually under an apostle).

> Do not neglect your gift, which was given you through a
> prophetic message when the body of elders (*presbuterion*)
> laid their hands on you. (1 Tim. 4:14)

Apparently Timothy received spiritual gifts through a prophecy when this group of elders, a presbytery, laid hands on him.

BISHOP

How did a chess piece come to be called a bishop? (Because it has to cross a *board* to get anywhere?) Did this chess piece seize its moniker from the fact that Catholic bishops at one time were powerful figures over territories? However, I'm only concerned with the use of the word in Scripture. Church tradition is only the hardened lava of men's ideas that has flowed down from Mount Opinion over time. Tradition is often the enemy of Scripture; Jesus constantly bumped up against the traditions of men.

Most churches make a title out of *bishop*. Face it: *bishop so-and-so* sounds like a dignitary; *pastor so-and-so* just sounds like a regular *so-and-so*! Also, the word is often used for a minister over other ministers. An overseer.

THE GREEK

The Greek word we get *bishop* or *overseer* from is *episkopos*. *Epi*—over; *skopos*—to watch. The basic meaning is *overseer*.

Since the pastor is the one overseeing the local church, he is the bishop.

....to all the saints at Phillippi, together with the <u>overseers</u> and deacons. (Phillipians 1:1b)

Obviously, he's talking about pastors and deacons here. Paul could have used any of the several synonyms for pastor here; he could have said "with the elders and deacons" or "with the shepherds and deacons." *Episkopoi* does fine. The very nature of a pastor's job is to *oversee*. A shepherd oversees the sheep.

Most denominations have church officials who oversee pastors. These people are usually called bishops. In the Catholic church, as mentioned before, the bishop is usually a prelate in flowing robes overseeing priests. But in the New Testament the *bishoping* is done by the pastor. Overseeing should be thought of as a function, not a rank. It is an aspect of shepherding. Every pastor is an overseer. And over the pastors was usually an apostle, not a *bishop*.

RESPONSIBILITIES OF OVERSEEING

Overseeing the flock involves protecting the flock. A lot of mutton gluttons are on the prowl.

But David said to Saul, "Your servant has been keeping his father's Sheep. When a lion or a bear came and carried off a sheep from the Flock, I went after it and rescued the sheep from its mouth. When it turned on me, I seized it by its hair, struck it and killed it. (1 Sam. 17: 34, 35)

I well remember when a woman of my congregation let me know she was going to another church. I wanted to be gracious. I didn't whine or put a guilt trip on her. I should have looked into the matter; she was being drawn into one of the many pseudo-Christian cults! (Don't offer to say grace when the wolf comes to eat your sheep!)

Keep watch over yourselves and all the flock of which the Holy Spirit has made you overseers (*episkopos*). Be shepherds of the church of God, which he bought with his own blood.

I know that after I leave, savage wolves will come in among you and will not spare the flock. (Acts 20:28, 29)

To be an overseer is to be on *wolf watch*. In politically-correct America, all religions are the same. The wolf has rights too (even the right to Little Red Riding Hood). You could dress up as a wolf and be more welcome in some liberal churches than a legit sheep.

THE *POIMEN*

Suppose you could roll all the functions of the local church leader into one term. *Eldering, bishoping,* overseeing, rod-and-staff work, saving the wounded, feeding the flock, bringing back those who wander astray, teaching, exhorting, opposing false doctrines, false teachers, and so on. What one term encompasses all these things? *Poimen.*

Poimen is the one Greek term that takes in all the above. *Poimen* simply means *shepherd!*

Of course, you're more familiar with the term *pastor.* Same thing.

Shepherds lead, feed, meet the need, heal those that bleed, oversee, teach, reach out, and stand over the flock as prominent leader–elder.

Why this term?

Why did God pick this term for the leader of the local church? Why not a more democratic term like *president?*

A president is one who presides. He stands over a group of people having a vote. He draws his power from below, from those he governs. A pastor should get his call from above, from the one he governs for. A president stands over a voting process that makes known the will of the people. A pastor should make known the will of God to the people. A president is limited by the people he governs; a pastor should be limited by God. A president is elected by people; a pastor should be selected by God, anointed by God, appointed by an apostle, or accepted by the people as God's appointee.

The reason this doesn't sound too democratic is because it isn't! Democracy is maybe the best thing for civil governments right now. However, *people rule* is just not a Scriptural way to govern the church.

Most churches that think they're democratic really aren't anyway. They're usually *boardocracies* or oligarchies–ruled by a small group within the church!

And why not a more autocratic term like *captain?* Because a shepherd is more about responsibility and caring than military-like authority. The term *poimen* captures the spirit and essence that God wants in a leader of his people. The shepherd is a gentle leader. He is more interested in the welfare of the sheep of God than in exercising his authority. But he must have authority because some situations demand it.

GOVERNMENT BY SHEPHERDS
God's government has always been by shepherds.

1) God himself is a shepherd (Psalm 23; Isaiah 40:11);
2) Jesus is the *good shepherd* (John 10:14a); *the great shepherd* (Heb. 13:20); *the Shepherd and Overseer of your souls* (1 Pet. 2:25); *the Chief Shepherd* (1 Pet. 5:4);
3) Moses was a shepherd (Ex. 3:1)
4) David was a shepherd (1 Sam.16:11).

The Egyptians despised shepherds; the Gentiles loved raw authority. But God chose the shepherd mode of leadership for his people–a humble leader exercising authority in love for the good of the sheep. A gentle *poimen*!

CHAPTER 7

ABLE TO TEACH

Pastors have an anointing to teach.

Now the overseer (pastor) must be...able to teach....(1Tim. 3:2)

This one phrase **disqualifies** the average lay-elder. The Greek word translated *able to teach* is *didaktikon*. It means *skilled in teaching*!

A baker is skilled in baking. Being able to pop open a can of biscuits and turn on the oven doth not a baker make you. A baker is not someone who gets an urge to bake something twice a year; he is skilled and knowledgeable in baking. (He makes his *dough* that way.) Baking is a baker's occupation.

Being able to stand up and talk 15 minutes at a prayer meeting doesn't qualify you as skilled in teaching. Neither does tripping over toddlers on Sunday morning with a quarterly in your hand mean you're a skilled teacher. To be skilled in teaching means you're able to feed the flock regularly!

Of course, we're talking about teaching the word! To be masterful at teaching history in high school while you dodge spit balls and juggle erasers doesn't get it. We're talking about knowing your way around the Bible.

> And the Lord's servant must not quarrel; instead, he must be kind to everyone, able to teach, (*didaktikon*) not resentful. (2 Tim. 2:24)

THE SHEPHERD'S MAIN WORK

The main work of a shepherd is to feed the flock. Jesus found a multitude of sheep who were "like sheep without a shepherd" (Mark 6:34). Jesus, the good shepherd, prioritized the first need of a flock. He fed them: "he began to teach them many things."

God's people are fed by teaching.

> Then I will give you shepherds after my own heart who will lead (or *feed*) you with knowledge and understanding. (Jer. 3:15)

This is how God's flock is fed. The Lord raises up pastors who regularly feed the flock on knowledge and understanding. This requires a pastor's anointing. Lay-elders, even if they are articulate, don't cut it.

If the ability to feed the flock regularly with good results is not there–the man is not an elder (pastor). In the Old Testament, the task of imparting knowledge fell to the priest:

> For the lips of a priest ought to preserve knowledge, and from his mouth men should seek instruction....(Mal. 2:7)

My people are destroyed from lack of knowledge. Because you have rejected knowledge, I also reject you as my priests....(Hosea 4:6)

Some churches have assistant pastors able to feed the flock, who are not recognized as elders, yet laymen who simply fill a chair at board meetings are elders! Let no one be called an elder who cannot feed the flock if it depended on him alone! (Or whose gift is being developed with that in mind.) And don't prop up a layman with an occasional teaching to qualify him as an elder. (Trying on a jersey doesn't make you a football player.)

The elders of Titus 1:5 (also called overseers in verse 7) had to be able to encourage others by sound teaching and to refute those who oppose it (vs. 9).

They must be silenced, because they are ruining whole households by teaching things they ought not to teach....(vs. 11)

Situations like this call for an overseer (pastor) skilled in teaching. (A fireman, not a neighbor with a garden hose!)

THE PASTOR'S TO DO LIST

Until I come, devote yourself to the public reading of Scripture, to preaching and to teaching. (1 Tim. 4:13)

I used to think that the difference in preaching and teaching was volume. If my Pentecostal pastor was talking to the Sunday school class in normal speaking tones, he was teaching. If he was in the pulpit and raised his voice level until the veins in his neck stood out, he was preaching! (The louder, the more anointed.)

Or you could distinguish preaching from teaching by the location of the necktie. If pastor loosened his tie and was sucking air, he was preaching. (Bless be the *tie* that doesn't bind.)

What we English speakers call *preaching* is usually exhortation. The Greek word for it is *parakaleo: para-* alongside, *kaleo*-to call. Picture an exhausted marathon runner nearing the finish. A friend (*parakletos*) runs up alongside and calls out encouragement: "Keep it up! You're almost there." To exhort is to encourage people to do what they already know to do.

The Holy Spirit himself is known as a *parakletos* or *paraclete*, *comforter* or *encourager*, from this word.

If the pastor is encouraging you to do what you already know to do, he's exhorting (regardless of volume).

On the other hand, the Greek word for *preach* is often *kerusso-*: to proclaim! To announce news. To herald. When Jesus preached (*kerusso*) to those spirits in prison in 1 Peter 3:19, he announced something to them. If these spirits were the fallen angels of Noah's day, he may have announced to them that he had provided salvation for the world they nearly destroyed. After all, he knew these angels personally. (We don't know what he announced, but he didn't give an altar call in Tartarus!)

Another Greek word is used to announce a message of good news. *Euaggelizo.* You guessed it; we get words like *evangelize, evangelist, evangel* from this word.

So, if I'm proclaiming the gospel to unbelievers, I'm preaching.

But the Greek word for teaching is *didasko.* This word means to impart information, to instruct, to explain, to show how. Jesus usually combined preaching with teaching.

Jesus went through all the towns and villages, teaching *(didasko)* in their synagogues, preaching (*kerusso*) the good news of the kingdom and healing every disease and sickness. (Matt. 9:35)

In short, to preach is to *proclaim*; to teach is to *explain;* and to exhort is to *exclaim*: "Let's do what we know to do!"

Timothy was told to read the word publicly, to exhort and to teach (1 Tim. 4:13). This kind of speaking grows healthy sheep. And healthy sheep reproduce sheep!

On occasion, the Holy Spirit may lead a pastor to evangelize on Sunday morning, to preach to the lost. But the general Scriptural rule is to exhort and teach the church–to grow the saints.

The multi-gifted apostle goes into an area, proclaims the gospel (usually with miracles), and then disciples converts with teaching, organizes churches, and appoints elders (pastors). And deacons, well, that's another chapter!

TEACHING AND BUSINESS ELDERS

Some people see two kinds of elders–teaching elders and business elders. The NIV's rendering of 1 Timothy 5:17 fuels this misunderstanding.

> The elders who direct the affairs of the church well are worthy of double honor, especially those whose work is preaching and teaching.

This seems to imply that there are some elders who preach and teach and some elders who administrate. Sure, and maybe there are worship elders and counseling elders and oversight elders and so on. To be consistent with the other verses on elders, the Greek in this verse should have been translated, *Especially those who work hard at preaching and teaching.* The very word *overseer* implies administration.

> If anyone sets his heart on being an overseer, he desires a noble task. (If anyone does not know how to manage his own family, how can he take care of God's church?) (1 Tim. 3:1b,5)

The Greek word for *manage* is *proestimi*– to rule! It's expected that overseers (pastors) manage the church. All overseers!

All elders teach and preach. All elders administrate. All elders exercise oversight. Shepherding is a multi-tasking job. A natural flock of sheep doesn't have one shepherd for feeding and another for counting, and so on. All shepherds have certain tasks; but different tasks don't require certain shepherds!

This is not to say that secretaries, deacons, and others may not help administrate. And the pastor certainly can't let management eat up his study and prayer time. But to exclude a pastor from administrative decisions is like telling a surgeon he can't cut!

OTHER TEACHERS

Of course, there are some teachers who are not pastors (1 Cor. 12:28, Eph. 4:11). There are traveling teachers, national teachers, and regional teachers. There are teachers who specialize in areas like faith or healing. Joyce Meyer has a very practical national teaching ministry. But while not all teachers are pastors, all pastors should be teachers. In fact, where Ephesians 4:11 mentions *pastors and teachers,* many think this refers to one office–the *pastor/teacher.*

Writing books can also be a teaching ministry. If it instructs, shows how, distinguishes, explains and informs, it's teaching.

CHAPTER 8

UNANIMOUS CONSENT

M any elder boards make decisions by unanimous consent. All have to agree for anything to pass.

With this decision-making machinery in place, one *no* outweighs a dozen *yeses*. One nay can delay or stay all progress on an issue. Under this arrangement one goat vote cancels the pastor and a table full of good men.

Unanimous consent is good. It's desirable. And it would work if church boards were populated by cherubim. But it's flesh and blood we work with in churches, sometimes anointed and sometimes not! What do you do on the *not* days?

Some churches think they're obligated by scripture to wrangle through the unanimous decision process. And sometimes guiding those present into agreement is like trying to herd cats in heat! Most pastors probably bind themselves to the unanimous agreement principle because of the apostles' conference in Acts 15.

THE JERUSALEM CONFERENCE

In the first century of the church, a conference of apostles and elders met at Jerusalem. The hot topic that convened this august meeting was the Law question: *Shall Gentiles (non-Jews) be required to keep the Law of Moses?* (Or can Christian Gentiles eat sausage biscuits at the McDonalds in Antioch?)

> Some men came down from Judea to Antioch and were teaching the brothers: "Unless you are circumcised, according to the custom taught by Moses, you cannot be saved." This brought Paul and Barnabas into sharp dispute and debate with them. So Paul and Barnabas were appointed, along with some other believers, to go up to Jerusalem to see the apostles and elders about this question. (Acts 15:9a, 10)

The Pharisees stood up on the *yes* side of this question (as *Phar* as we see, we're the only ones right). *Circumcise them!* Cut them in but hand them a book of Law. Require them to keep all 613 rules of the Old Testament (which none of the Pharisees were keeping).

Leaping to the negative side of the question was Peter:

> He (God) made no distinction between us and them....Now then, why do you try to test God by putting on the necks of the disciples a yoke that neither we nor our fathers were able to bear. (vss. 9a, 10)

To paraphrase Peter, *We couldn't keep the law, so why require the Gentiles to keep it?*

After the *Simon says* session, Paul and Barnabas took the floor:

> The whole assembly became silent as they listened to Barnabas and Paul telling about the miraculous signs and wonders God had done among the Gentiles through them. (vs. 12)

After the Law question had been *Peter'd* and *Paul'd* and *Pharisee'd*, do we have unanimous consent?

No vote is recorded. But this group did seem to come to unanimous agreement.

> Then the apostles and elders with the whole church, decided to choose Some of their own men and send them to Antioch with Paul and Barnabas....(vs. 22a)

Apparently the whole church unanimously agreed that Gentiles not be put under Moses' Law. (Head for Hardee's!)

So, some find here a guiding principle: Church leaders should unanimously agree on all decisions!

'Scuse me. This is a good example; but there's nothing here that says all church decisions should be unanimously agreed to.

WHO DECIDED THE ISSUE?

Notice: a vote did not decide this issue. After all sides were heard, an overseer brought down the gavel. James gave his judgement and the matter was settled.

When they finished, James spoke up: "Brothers, listen to me....It is my judgement, therefore that we should not make it difficult for the Gentiles who are turning to God. Instead we should write to them, telling them to abstain from food polluted by idols, from sexual immorality, from the meat of strangled animals and from blood. (vss. 13, 19, 20)

Notice also that when the official letter went out from the conference, it represented the opinion of the apostles and elders:

With them they sent the following letter: The apostles and elders, your brothers, to the Gentile believers in Antioch, Syria and Cilicia: Greetings. (vs. 23)

Other believers may have been heard at the conference, but the final word of the conference was by the overseer. God governs by shepherds.

The Jerusalem conference settled the issue for that time, but Paul battled the Law question for years (Rom. 3:21, 24; 6:14; 7:4, 6; 8:2-4; Gal. 2:15, 16, 19; 3:10-13; 5:2-4, 16 just to name some of the texts). Even today, Law cults abound. And many Christians are confused as to whether to keep the

Old Testament laws or not. I was startled at a Charismatic conference to hear a minister blurt out that we ought to keep the Old Testament laws. *It's also the Bible.* But that's a subject for a different time.

WHEN SAINTS DON'T SYNC!
Unity is always to be had if possible.

How good and pleasant it is for brothers to dwell together in unity! It is like the precious oil poured on the head, Running down on the beard....For there the Lord bestows his blessing, even life forevermore. (Psalm 133:1, 2a, 3)

Oil flows where there's unity (the Spirit). And sometimes only the Spirit can bring unity. Indeed only the Holy Spirit could have merged those diverse factions at the Jerusalem conference into a consensus (like tossing Irish Catholics and Protestants into a blender).

But sometimes the saints just won't sync. Unanimous agreement should always be reached for, but sometimes is out of reach:

1) A brother is not walking in the Spirit (Gal.5:15);
2) A controlling spirit positions itself on the board;
3) Pride pulls up a chair;
4) A board member comes in with a faction's agenda (or his wife's);
5) Or, people just need fresh batteries in their hearing aids.

And, of course, the devil never misses a board meeting–in case opportunities present themselves! If Thomas Edison had to work with some boards, you'd be reading this by candlelight!

APOSTLES DISAGREE

Even the apostles Paul and Barnabas couldn't reach agreement on one occasion.

Sometime later Paul said to Barnabas, "Let us go back and visit the brothers in all the towns where we have preached the word of the Lord and see how they are doing." Barnabas wanted to take John, also called Mark, with them, but Paul did not think it wise to take him, because he had deserted them in Pamphylia.... they had such a sharp disagreement that they parted company. Barnabas took Mark and sailed for Cyprus, but Paul chose Silas and left, commended by the brothers to the grace of the Lord.

Captured in Scripture, an apostolic argument! (Like overhearing Mother Theresa cuss!) And these two great men didn't even agree to disagree agreeably. And neither would give in. Barnabas drops off the radar after this so some think he's the one who ran through the YIELD sign. But who knows? Maybe Paul got cantankerous. On extremely rare occasions, even *I* have gotten out of the Spirit. (So my wife says.)

THE PETE AND PAUL BRAWL

Would you believe that the heavyweights Peter and Paul clashed on an occasion?

Peter had accepted the fact that Gentiles could be saved without being circumcised and keeping the Law of Moses—until some prominent Jews came down from Jerusalem. Then Pete lapsed back into his Jew view; he began to separate himself from the uncircumcised Gentiles like old Southern whites refusing to eat with blacks. (No Gentiles at the bagel table please!)

> Before certain men came down from James (the apostle at Jerusalem), he used to eat with the Gentiles. But when they arrived, he began to draw back and separate himself from the Gentiles because he was afraid of those who belonged to the circumcision group. The other Jews joined him in his hypocrisy, so that by their hypocrisy even Barnabas was led astray. (vss. 12, 13)

Remember, it was Peter who had first preached the gospel to the Gentiles (Acts 10)! It was Peter with John who laid hands on those half-Gentile Samaritans to receive the Holy Spirit (Acts 8). He advocated for the Gentiles at the Jerusalem conference; he had signed on to the apostolic letter releasing non-Jews from keeping Moses' Law (Acts 15). Now Pete appears to be in full retreat.

Enter the doctrinal pit bulldog, Paul.

When Peter came to Antioch, I opposed him to his face, because he was clearly in the wrong. (Gal. 2:11)

No problem with plain language here. This was a clash of titans. Possibly the two greatest apostles having a set-to.

Paul wasn't about to unanimously agree with this Hebrew hypocrisy. You don't sacrifice *right* on the altar of unanimous agreement. When the right crowd heads the wrong way, somebody needs to stand up and speak up.

UNANIMOUS AGREEMENT AND MOSES

Moses was the meekest man on earth. He easily out-meeked the runner-up, whoever that was. You'd think a man like Moses would walk around with *I agree* written on his forehead. But Moses came up with a key *no* at the right time and saved the nation. Had Moses bent to the raucous crowd, the Israelites would have gone back to Egypt, been absorbed into the Egyptian culture, died with garlic on their breaths, and been lost as a nation with unmarked graves. (Going back on God can be a *grave* mistake!)

THE TWELVE SPIES

A little background: twelve CIA types were sent to spy out the land of Canaan.

The Lord said to Moses, "Send some men to explore the land of Canaan....From each ancestral tribe send one its leaders. So at the Lord's command Moses sent them out. (Num. 13:2, 3a)

Israel's future could hang on this committee's report. Actually, they shouldn't have been deciding *whether* to invade the land; God had already decided that. They were to gather intelligence (the intelligent thing to do). This trip should have simply affirmed that what God had promised about the land was true. But how often do church committees get into matters that are not on their agendas?

This committee should have grabbed pom poms when they arrived home and started cheerleading. "Rah! Everything he said was true!"

Remember, these men had seen miracles. They had seen the Red Sea stacked up like quivering walls of jello; water flowed from a rock; bread fell from heaven every morning, and a cloud pillar led them like a divine cursor pointing the way and functioned as a supernatural night light! But a bad heart leads to a wrong head (or vice-versa).

Ten of the committee positioned themselves against the promises of God with a negative report.

> But the men who had gone up with him said, "We can't attack these people; they are stronger than we are." And they spread among the Israelites a bad report....(Num. 13:31, 32a)

Their unbelief spread through the camp like a rumor on the stock market floor.

> That night all the people of the community raised their voices and wept aloud. (14:1)

Suddenly, public opinion turned against Moses like a weathervane turning on the first gust of a storm.

All the Israelites grumbled against Moses and Aaron, and the whole assembly (so much for majority rule) said to them, "If only we had died In Egypt." (14:2a)

However, two members of the spy committee refused unanimous consent. Joshua and Caleb issued a minority report.

Joshua (same name as Jesus) son of Nun and Caleb ("dog"–calls to mind dogged determination), who were among those who had explored the land, tore their clothes and said, "Their protection is gone, but the Lord is with us. Do not be afraid of them." (14:6, 9b)

That bit of positive thinking (based on faith) almost got the faithful stoned! Moses could have meekly gone along. Weren't the people determined to go back to Egypt anyway? Wasn't he a stone's throw away from losing his position?

Democracy or unanimous consent here would have consigned Israel to eternal anonymity as an Egyptian sub-culture.

What's needed is a shepherd with a backbone.

Imagine flying a plane democratically. Some of the passengers decide in-flight that they want to go to a different destination. Shall we let the passengers vote? While passengers do have rights, these rights are limited. They include the right to get on and get off the plane (but not in-flight). When passengers board the plane, it is understood they are in agreement with the route the plane is taken (unless it's hijacked). Passengers do not organize committees to govern the plane in flight.

If I can't agree with a pastor's vision, I may talk with him. I may pray for him. But if I can't connect with way the church is going, I'll get out of the way. And I'll get out of the way the right way! I won't start a faction, start a rival home group, or try to draw others away from the church. I don't want Miriam's leprosy! (See Numbers 12.)

CHAPTER 9

BOARD STIFF!

Most American institutions are *boardocracies.* Church government, too, is usually measured in *board feet.* An elder board or deacon board or board of directors directs the selection of other boards and committees to direct the work of other boards and committees.

If you've read this far without tossing this book, you probably think I'm against all boards. (Better to walk the plank than to cross the board!) You assume I'm going to ban all boards until the second coming (until you and Jesus and Paul make up the elder board for the millennial reign).

You're wrong for that! Actually, boards are a good thing. (Even Michael Jordan scores points by bouncing things off a board!) In fact, boards are probably necessary in most churches to accommodate the American mentality and to neutralize *Jim Jones phobia.*

AMERICAN *GOVERNMENTALITY*

Americans see the church as a dime-size democracy or a postage stamp republic. The congregation represents the people, the board is congress, and the pastor is the president.

The American form of government is overlaid onto the church.

God forbid that I sound un-American. Democracy is the best form of government for nations in this present time. And there is no country I would leave America for. But democracy is not New Testament government for the church.

By the way, a democracy is only as good as the character of the majority! When an immoral majority surfaces, you may find yourself in a *demon*ocracy!

By selecting a shepherd form of government, God excluded democracy. Shepherds are not elected– they're selected. They don't run for office; they run because they have an office. They're anointed and appointed by the Holy Spirit, and an apostle or presbytery. Of course, these days when there are few real apostles, many pastors simply start up churches and by virtue of that are elders. Of course, denominations usually have evolved systems of placing pastors.

But true biblical government is without ballot boxes, polls, or referendums. It is government by a gentle, strong leader who carries the sheep next to his heart. (And that sometimes causes heartburn.)

To say that the church is not a democracy is not to say the congregation never has a say. There are times when the collective opinion of the church should be in front of the decision-makers. But more on that later.

INPUT

David conferred with each of his officers, the commanders of thousands and commanders of hundreds. (1 Chron.13:1)

After consulting the people, Jehoshaphat appointed men to sing to the Lord and to praise him for the splendor of his holiness....(1 Chron. 20:21)

Pastors need input! Boards can be a well of wisdom to draw from. Often, the brains for a project may not rest on the shepherd's shoulders. Another head at the table may hold the expertise needed. A banker may have the financial savvy. (It's always good to have people you can *bank* on.) A builder will have construction know-how.

Plans fail for lack of counsel, But with many advisors they succeed. (Prov.15:22)

The best shepherd's brains come with blind spots. A wise man will listen to a fool though a fool won't listen to a wise man. A wise pastor is a listening pastor!

MORE INPUT

There are times when the input of the whole church may be sought. After David conferred with his commanders, he turned to the whole assembly:

He then said to the whole assembly of Israel, "if it seems good to you And if it is the will of the Lord our God....Let us bring the ark of our God back to us...." (1 Chron. 13:2a, 3b)

Often the Holy Spirit will lead a pastor to involve the whole congregation in a decision–especially a building program. (Unless you've got room in your budget for a church payment!) Good will and favor can be often be garnered by consultation with those who must share the obligation.

David was careful in this particular situation to expose other minds to his project. He was going to bring the ark of God to Jerusalem. The last time he tried to bring the ark, he didn't read the instructions! Only priests carry the ark; you don't load it on an ox cart like a dead cow (no *cart blanche*). The Philistines got away with that because of their ignorance. When you could know, God expects you to know. David should have gone to a priest's website and briefed himself on *arkeology*.

The men of Bethshemesh learned you don't peek into the ark either (1 Sam. 6:19). When they removed the blood-sprinkled lid, the mercy seat, from over the commandments (broken law–sin), the death angel tapped them on the shoulder! Sin equals death if not covered by the blood (atonement, Rom. 6:23).

And never grab the ark! When you get to heaven, ask Uzzah why (2 Sam. 6:6, 7). It was the irreverent handling of the ark by Uzzah that had broken up the first ark journey, and now David was nervous about this second try to bring the ark to Jerusalem. He carefully gathered input; he consulted. If David had done his homework the first time, it wouldn't have rained on his ark parade. But don't lose sight of this fact: David consulted, but the decision was his. If the commanders had said, "No," David could have still said, "Go!" He could have given the green light even if the assembly was blinking caution. At any point David could have decided to put an ark detail in the road.

I'm not implying that a pastor should have a king's authority. But he should have veto power over committees and boards. He should cultivate unity and court consensus, but the final decision should be his. We grant even a little league coach the latitude to make decisions. Shouldn't a pastor have at least that much authority?

A pastor must be positioned to take a stand if he has to, even against the board's and the congregation's wishes. Remember, the congregation wanted to go back to Egypt! But bishop Moses took a stand.

Of course, as we say elsewhere, the pastor must take responsibility for his decisions. Empty pews don't pay bills. If it's the right thing to do, do it and trust God to get you through it!

BOARD LIMITS

Board may be useful indeed. But boards should be limited:

1) Boards should advise, not direct;

2) Pastors should select boards–boards shouldn't select pastors;

3) Pastors should fire board members–boards should not be able to fire pastors.

YES BOARDS

Some pastors, like the chess piece called the *bishop*, slide across the board issue by appointing family and cronies to the board. There's nothing wrong with having family and friends on the board, but if you create a 100% rubber stamp board, you deprive yourself of valuable input. If you populate the board with people who parrot you, you cancel variety of opinion. (Not that creating a board of *no* people speeds progress either).

If you've got an *echo* board, you're probably missing controversy but some wisdom with it. A board should be comfortable to disagree with you and comfortable when you reject their opinion (agree to disagree agreeably). Don't slap a *rebel* label on others when they differ with you in a right spirit.

REPRESENTATION

It's to the pastor's advantage to have different groups–seniors, youth, women, and so on–represented on the board. And sometimes there are people who don't represent any particular group but who have distinguished themselves by their spirit or knowledge. However, contentious people, rebellious types, non-tithers, gossips, and real carnal types who will seek to be on the board are administrative hemorrhoids! Knowingly appointing some people to the board is the equivalent of self-flagellation!

ROTATING BOARDS

Some pastors defer to a rotating advisory board. (*Rotating* here doesn't mean going around in circles.) A rotating system gives the opportunity to rotate bad eggs off the board. However, depending on how you're set up, you can obligate yourself to rotate good eggs off the board too. It may be wise to keep your system of acquiring board members on a trial basis for a while. Call it an *experiment* for lack of a more spiritual term.

Don't forget to call the board an *advisory board.* Put the word *advisory* in print somewhere. Let board members know they'll probably rotate off the board at some point. (Write it on their foreheads with a permanent marker!) Don't commit rashly to any system.

WHO HOLDS THE FLUTE?

The bottom line on the pastor/board game is who can fire whom. If the board can fire you, they play the flute and you dance. If you teach on tithes and several non-tithing board members pick up the flute, get on your toes! (Or back up faster than a lobster leaving a seafood restaurant.)

Of course, we all like to think our church is not like that. Yeah, but things can change faster than a chameleon having a hot flash. Strive for the ideal, but be real. I've seen too much stuff that couldn't happen happen to people it couldn't happen to. (Be prepared for *stuff that can't happen!*)

If your pastor and board have gotten along blissfully with no rules for a while, wonderful! May you make it to the rapture without rupturing. But if one day an "X" factor should take a seat on the board, a clear understanding in writing could be a fire extinguisher on the wall.

BOARD TO DEATH!

But what about the pastor who's inherited a tough board situation? The board called you to the church. (And now they're calling you other things.)

You can pray for things to change. You can pray new blood into your situation– new board members. The Holy Spirit may say "Wait it out"; you may need the faith of Abraham and the patience of Job if he does. You'll have to hang on, hang in, hang out, hang loose, hang tough, and pray you don't hang it up before you're hanged! But if God said do it, he can give you favor. (And if you have grand kids in the ministry, you'll have lots of stories!)

Some board members may have to die out. (You can't pray for that, though.) Look for the Holy Spirit's leading. Make sure you have the mind of God if you start a new church; innocent people can get damaged. I know from my own experience, though, that a bad board can sometimes be God's midwife for a new church!

MY BOARD EXPERIENCE

At this writing, I serve on the board at my church. My pastor has an open mind and listens to everyone. I express my opinion freely and often. (My jaw is sprayed with WD40.) But I respect the pastor's right to make the final call. If I eventually can't agree with the vision of the church, I'll try to make an exit with no wake. Having had my share of trouble from board members, this is my shining opportunity to be a board member and cause no problem. I have no desire to cause a man of God worry. This pastor's been gracious to me. How many pastors welcome an ex-pastor and give him opportunity to minister?

FINALLY, KEEP IT SIMPLE!

So, finally, pastor, keep it simple. Have a board, but call it an advisory board. And be a humble servant; serve the board like Christ, the servant leader. But like an honest umpire in a baseball game, make the call when you have to! Back up when you're wrong; stand when you're right.

CHAPTER 10

RESPECT FOR THE OFFICE

Many pastors could duet with the comedian Rodney Dangerfield: *I don't get no respect!*

In a society that's so far gone it parades its decadence on the Jerry Springer show, there's always less respect for authority. But even before now, church people have traditionally seen the pastor as a church employee: a hireling, a paid emcee, a functionary, a nickel-and-nose counter, a bought figurehead, or a necessary liaison between the church and the community.

To some, the pastor is the elected president. He presides. He shepherds the decision-making minds to an agreement. He may or may not have a vote.

To some, the pastor is the counselor. You can confide in him without your secret showing up on a deacon's web site. He dispenses free advice like a flower girl tripping down a church aisle and scattering petals.

In some churches, the bishop is the anointed flunky. He mechanics the widow's car. If the plumbing in the fellowship hall gets clogged up for the umpteenth time, pastor gets the call. (To have a pastor who can fix plumbing is a *pipe* dream!)

Besides all this, a good pastor is an administrator. He can balance figures like a juggler on uppers!

Pastor has more hats than a Red Skelton comedy routine. He's as versatile as an ambidextrous person with a monkey wrench in each hand. The man of God struggles along with a flock of trouble, a lamb under each arm, goats chewing on his pants leg, wolves nipping at his heels, tippy-toeing around sheep manure, adjusting columns of figures and trying not to step on deacons' or elders' toes at the same time. (A tight wire-walker on a greased wire has it easier!)

THE PASTOR'S AUTHORITY

A pastor can't go down to the Christian bookstore and buy a pastor's badge of authority. Authority must be given by the Holy Spirit and accepted by the people.

Someone has said that authority comes from feeding. As people receive teaching that brings about change in their lives, respect for the man of God grows. Sheep come to rely on a shepherd that is building them with teaching as he walks them through their experiences. When people come to know you seek their good, they find themselves assenting to your leadership.

When a pastor has to demand respect, it may be lacking for a good reason. It's hard for people not to respect a pastor when he sincerely ministers to their needs. Of course, there's occasionally a rabid sheep so eaten up with rebellion he's beyond connecting with trust.

PASTORS GIVE AN ACCOUNT!

A pastor deserves respect because he is responsible for God's people.

Obey your leaders and submit to their authority. They keep watch over you as men who must give an account. Obey them so their work will be a joy, not a burden, for that would be of not advantage to you. (Heb. 13:17)

A pastor having to give account for his people? The church minutes probably don't include that in his job description. In most places, the church considers itself responsible for the pastor. But if someone is lost spiritually because of a pastor's negligence, he will be called to account for it at the judgement. (I'm not saying the pastor will be lost for this, but accountable.)

But hold it! If the pastor is accountable for you, then he's responsible to speak into your life. He doesn't control you (witchcraft), but he must warn you when you're doing a spiritual bungee jump with a frayed cord!

One time when I was pastoring, an idea for Sunday's teaching came out of the clear blue: "Speak on Jehovah's Witnesses." Why? There was no JW activity going on that I could see. Why interrupt the teaching series that I was doing? Nevertheless, I obeyed. Later that Sunday I found one of the brothers slightly upset with me. He had been up the JW *Watchtower*! That Sunday morning teaching short-circuited his cult venture! I was just the megaphone the Holy Spirit used.

How many times do pastors hear, "Pastor, you preached on exactly what I needed"?

He must hold firmly to the trustworthy message as it has been taught, so that he can encourage others by sound doctrine and refute those who oppose it. (Tit. 1:9)

Keep watch over yourselves and all the flock of which the Holy Spirit has made you overseers. Be shepherds of the church of God, which he bought with his own blood. (Acts 20:28)

A pastor who looks out for your safety and welfare deserves your respect. Listen to him!

THE "O" WORD

Obey your leaders and submit to their authority....(Heb. 13:17)

It seems nobody feels they should have to obey anybody anymore. Princess Diana excised the "O" word out of the royal marriage ceremony. The idea that wives should obey husbands has dinosaur status. Former president Jimmy Carter assailed Southern Baptists for holding on to the archaic idea that women should submit to their husband's leadership. (We can't have *archaic* and eat it too!) What pastor would dare teach that pastors should be obeyed? (Or what visiting speaker would take up that exhortation?)

Yet there it is in black and white, "Obey your leaders."

It's really not a hard thing to obey a good pastor; he won't abuse you. Any instruction he gives will be for your good. He won't quarrel or force his will on you.

> And the Lord's servant must not quarrel; instead, he must be kind to everyone, able to teach, not resentful. (2 Tim. 2:24)

When an anointed pastor speaks into your situation and you've turned your hearing aid down, the onus falls on you. Only fools are offended when a lifeguard whistles them away from the no swim zone. Does it abridge anybody's rights for a coach to correct his player? If a pastor is really wrong in your opinion, and sometimes he is, then respectfully, prayerfully, and carefully decline to follow his advice. You can elect to respect even if you decide to reject the counsel.

THE ROD

A shepherd carried a rod (Ps. 23:4). A rod was for necessary correction for the good of the sheep.

> Therefore, rebuke them sharply, so that they will be sound in the faith and will pay no attention to Jewish myths or to the commands of those who reject the truth. (Tit. 1:13b, 14)

When you stray, the rod may come down in the form of a stern warning. Sometimes you hear the rod in an anointed teaching. The Holy Spirit often cloaks himself in a gentle admonition. Words of wisdom may be transported in casual conversation. A person can feel remorse or resentment or concern. But whether you feel stroked, stoked, or provoked, give a respectful hearing.

Using a rod doesn't require harshness; it does require seriousness. The function going down is correction. We don't like to be corrected. Correction is not on the list of the church's ten most fun things. But there have been people who've been saved from divorce, disaster, disappointment, and maybe death because of correction.

We're not talking about pastoral abuse. Even the rod is to be used in a right spirit. But it is to be used. Receive correction rightly; it may save your hide.

And even if you don't agree with the pastor after weighing his words carefully, agree to disagree agreeably. At least put his counsel on the back burner. Make sure you're not hardened because of rebellion or pride or wanting your own way. Maintain respect.

A SPECIAL KIND OF LEADER

God picked the term *shepherd* or *pastor* because it characterizes a special kind of leader. It differs from the Gentile idea of leader.

You know that the rulers of the Gentiles lord it over them, and their high officials exercise authority over them. (Matt. 20:25b)

The Greek word translated *lord it over them* is *katakurieuo*–to overpower or have power over. That word would send a crawler across the bottom of the Greek mind–raw, unquestioned authority! A dictator's baton is imbedded in the term.

Paul employs this term in 2 Corinthians 1:24: "Not that we lord it over your faith, but we work with you for your joy...."

Abusive, dominating leadership is forbidden to pastors.

Be shepherds of God's flock that is under your care, serving as overseers--not because you must, but because you are willing, as God wants you to be; not greedy for money, but eager to serve, not <u>lording it over</u> those entrusted to you, but being examples to the flock. (1 Peter 5:2, 3)

The same Greek word is used here for *lording it over.* Pastors should be gentle, not using their authority for personal advantage. A pastor who rules with a gentle but firm hand will gain the respect of people inside and outside his church.

CHAPTER 11

WHEN THE PASTOR GETS WEIRD!

Okay, so the shepherd's in charge. But what if he gets weird? Do we keep coming but sit near the exit?

At this writing, the pastor of a huge church in Georgia is being sued by some women of his congregation. According to them, pastor took advantage of them sexually. But can you impeach a pastor?

Catholic bishops are meeting about this time also. Seems a small army claims to have been molested by priests. (Most were young boys at the time.)

So what about pastors who raid the treasury and run off with the treasurer, or who disrupt the harmony of the church by exiting with the piano player, or whose antics top those of a tom cat on Viagra? I heard of one pastor who abandoned his family and checked out with a homosexual lover.

Why not keep the pastor under the watchful eye of a board? Why not legislate some rules against David walking on his housetop while Bathsheba is bathing in her back yard?

SIN WILL FIND A WAY

No form of church government can prevent sexual sin. Whether the pastor is over the board, or the board is over the pastor, somebody can go overboard! (Stuff happens!) By the way, it's not always the pastor splitting with the church secretary; sometimes it's a board member going south with the pastor's wife. Pastor's wives are vulnerable when pastors are just too busy. (Some pastors can't say "no" to praying the opening prayer at an atheists' convention!)

You can't sin-proof a church! You can't install a *McAfee Virus Sex Scan*, for the collective church leadership mind. There is no spiritual *firewall* against fornication. Each person is responsible to seek God and say *no mas* to the devil for himself. Sin can't be structured out of the church. There is no Teflon policy.

But what to do when the pastor does get weird? What if the bishop gets into a cult? What if he is seduced by punk rockers and comes in with his hair in green spikes? (There goes the AARP crowd.) What if your elder takes you back under Old Testament law and outlaws ham at the church supper? (Or chitterlings even....)

What if the shepherd gets into *Shepherding*–that 80's error where leaders controlled people's lives. Or frankly, what to do if the pastor gets into something like drugs (goes to *pot*). Are we bound to follow this man when it's obvious his cheese has slipped off his cracker? Are we helpless passengers on the bus?

Sure we respect the pastor's office. But every truth has its extreme. When the captain starts foaming at the mouth, abandon ship!

THE DAVID PRINCIPLE

When David was young, his king was Saul. Saul was anointed by God to be king. He had oil poured on him by the prophet Samuel. He was selected by God, not elected by the people. But king Saul took offense at the lyrics in the latest "rock" song: David killed Goliath with a *rock,* remember?

....the women came out from all the towns of Israel to meet Saul with singing and dancing, with joyful songs and with tambourines and lutes. As they danced they sang: "Saul has slain his thousands, and David his tens of thousands." (1 Sam. 18:6b, 7)

Plainly, some unknown composer never took Political Correctness 101. You don't praise a Medal of Honor winner over the king.

Saul was very angry; this refrain galled him...."What more can he get but the kingdom?" (1 Sam. 18:8)

Jealousy coupled with fear and hatred can open the door for a demon.

The next day an evil spirit from God came forcefully upon Saul....*(10a)*

An "evil spirit from God" simply means that God allowed an evil spirit to come on Saul. God removed his protection because of Saul's envy and rebellion. Rebellion seems to parallel the occult and draw the curiosity of demons. This demon first came upon Saul in chapter 16 after he willfully disobeyed God in chapter 15:

> Then the word of the Lord came to Samuel: "I am grieved because I have made Saul king, because he has turned away from me and has not carried out my instructions."

> For rebellion is like the sin of divination....(1 Sam. 15:10, 11a, 23a)

> Now the Spirit of the Lord had departed from Saul, and an evil spirit from the Lord tormented him. (1 Sam. 16:14)

This is the first case in the Bible of a person having a demon (or a demon having a person). This shows the danger of rebellion. Rebellion draws demons like witchcraft because witchcraft is rebellion. In fact, when you participate in the occult, you participate in the devil's rebellion against God. You violate the first commandment principle by having anything to do with other gods (demons).

EXIT STAGE LEFT

Put yourself in David's boots. Saving the king's rear has now put you in arrears in the relationship because some song writer topped the chart with your "giant" effort. And now your boss has a demon. What's next?

> While David was playing the harp....Saul had a spear in his hand and he hurled it saying to himself, "I'll pin David to the wall." (1 Sam.18:10b, 11a)

The spear missed but David got the point! (Never let your boss hang your coat up while you're still in it.) The demonized king is now set on downsizing his staff, and David doesn't have seniority.

Is it okay for David to rebel now?

David could take Saul; he had just killed a giant. And he could claim self-defense (or that he's just returning Saul's spear). But even extreme circumstances don't justify rebellion. David took the better option:

> ....David eluded him twice. (1 Sam. 18:11b)

After this Saul tried to assassinate David indirectly, using the Philistines. He offered his daughter Michal to David for 100 Philistine foreskins. Knowing, of course, that the Philistines wouldn't take kindly to being whittled on, Saul thought he was assigning David to certain death.

David delivered the delicate dowry. (Tough on the Philistines though.)

IS EVEN-STEVEN ALWAYS GOD GIVEN?

....a cave was there, and Saul went in to relieve himself.
David and his men were far back in the cave. The men
said, "This is the day the Lord spoke of when he said to
you, 'I will give your enemy into your hands for you to
deal with as you wish.'" Then David crept unnoticed and
cut off a corner of Saul's robe. (1 Sam. 243b, 4)

What an opportunity! David could have relieved himself
of Saul. Saul is in the position of someone sitting in an
outhouse with a shotgun coming through the door.

And David's men remind him again of God's promise!
Wasn't it prophesied that Saul would die? So, is it rebellion
if it's prophecy? (Don't we have to do our part to fulfill
prophecy?)

Can you believe it? David was conscience-stricken for
just trimming Saul's robe!

"The Lord forbid that I should do such a thing to my
master, the Lord's anointed, or lift my hand against him;
for he is the anointed of the Lord." (1 Sam. 24:6)

It appeared that David had a God-given right to carve Saul
like a Thanksgiving turkey. (Don't we all at times want to
carve our turkeys?) David's fugitive friends stood nodding
amen. But the man of God chose to do right when he could
have done what could pass as right. (David is no politician.)

COMING AGAINST THE LORD'S ANOINTED!

It's as serious as a train wreck to come against the Lord's anointed. In recent years I've sent several apology letters for carving Saul's hemline a time or two. My old attitudes have come back and paraded across my psyche like stolen chickens. I don't think there are any cut garments left in my closet.

David again spared Saul in chapter 26 of First Samuel:

So David and Abishai went to the army by night, and there was Saul asleep inside the camp with his spear stuck in the ground near his head....

Abishai said to David, "Today God has delivered your enemy into your hands. Now let me pin him to the ground with one thrust of my spear; I won't strike him twice. (vss. 7, 8)

This is an even better Saul-elimination situation! Again David is told that God has delivered Saul into his hands. And Abishai stands with a cocked spear; he can be the instrument. David can say that Saul didn't die by his hand. Abishai was just fulfilling prophecy.

No go. Again David saves Saul's life.

But David said to Abishai, "Don't destroy him! Who can lay a hand on the Lord's anointed and not be guiltless? As surely as the Lord lives," he said, "The Lord himself will strike him; either his time will come and he will die, or he will go into battle and perish. But the Lord forbid that I should lay a hand on the Lord's Anointed." (vss. 9a, 10, 11b)

Saul deserves to die. But David keeps getting this "pop up" on his screen about the Lord's anointed–"Do not touch my anointed ones; do my prophets no harm" (1 Chron. 16:22).

Eventually David's word, "or he will go into battle and perish," came true. Saul committed suicide after defeat in battle (1 Sam. 30). The sword that sought David did a "U Turn" into Saul's gut!

PARACHUTEOLOGY

If the pastor gets weird, bail out!

Don't stay on board and crash with a pastor who's downloaded a virus.

If pastor has shacked up with his secretary because "my wife wouldn't cook my favorite dessert," don't buy that. If that big sucking sound is the church's money going into video poker machines–re-direct your tithe. Don't let some teaching on extreme submission torque you into supporting weirdness!

But don't rebel! If there is an apostle or presbytery over the pastor, inform him. If the pastor will listen to responsible people who genuinely have his interest at heart, good. But never organize a mutiny. Don't orchestrate a rebellion. David maintained respect for the anointed office over him even while dodging spears. If you can't obey an obviously wayward pastor, get out of the way!

But if you rebel, welcome to Saul's club. Rebellion against a rebellious leader paints you with the same brush.

Believe it or not–Some people think this belongs in the *Ripley* category–God himself can remove or reprove one of his leaders! Bail out if the situation really demands it (with your tithe in your back pocket). But don't pollute your spirit with anger and bitterness trained against one of God's finest. Dodge the spear, do what you're honestly responsible to do, and trust God for the outcome. Let God correct his man.

CHAPTER 12

EARLY CHURCH STRUCTURE

Again, in Acts 20, Paul summons the elders of the Ephesian church.

> From Miletus, Paul sent to Ephesus for the elders of the church. (vs. 17)

s this church of Ephesus one big local church in Ephesus? Or does *church* here represent all the local churches of that city?

Since there were no denominations then, *which* church of Ephesus is no problem.

Were there small churches scattered over large cities or regions? Obviously, there were no mega-churches. There were no huge buildings yet. (Because building fund envelopes hadn't been invented yet.)

HOUSE CHURCHES
Churches met in houses (and possibly courtyards of houses).

Greet also the church that meets at their house....(Rom. 16:5a)

Aquila and Priscilla greet you warmly in the Lord, and so does the church that meets at their house. (1 Cor. 16:19b)

Give my greetings to the brothers a Laodicea, and to Nympha and the church in her house. (Col. 4:15)

To Apphia our sister, to Archippus our fellow soldier and to the church That meets in your home. (Philemon 1:2)

These were not home groups. They were churches that met in houses over the city or area. Transportation was limited (homeward-bound donkeys being the fastest); so contact between churches may have been slight.

IS THERE A LEADER IN THE HOUSE?
Each house church had a leader over it. This leader would be a shepherd. He would also be called an *elder* or *overseer.* (A point this book belabors!) These elders are the men that Paul sent for in Acts 20:17.

There were also local churches scattered over the city of Philippi.

Paul and Timothy, servants of Christ Jesus, to all the saints in Christ Jesus at Philippi, together with the overseers and deacons. (Phil. 1:1)

Here the pastors are simply called *overseers*. And, of course, I can't miss an opportunity to say that the overseers of Philippi are the same as the elders of Ephesus–pastors!

OVERSEEING THE OVERSEERS

Over the pastors of a city or region was an apostle. For instance, Paul oversaw all the cities of Crete (Titus 1:5). Since transportation was mostly by foot and Paul had several regions and cities to oversee, Paul would delegate authority over an area to a trusted brother. (Deputy apostle? Apostle in training?)

> The reason I left you in Crete (Titus) was that you might straighten out what was left unfinished and appoint elders in every town, as I directed you. (Titus 1:5)

Plainly, Titus had authority to appoint elders. This was delegated directly from the apostle.

In Acts 14:23, Paul and Barnabas appointed elders in every church.

> Paul and Barnabas appointed elders for them in every church and, with prayer and fasting, committed them to the Lord in whom they had put their trust.

Apostles appoint pastors; get it?

Another apostle designee was Timothy. Timothy was authorized to ordain pastors (1 Tim. 5:22); hear accusations against pastors (1 Tim. 5:19); correct pastors (1 Tim. 5:20);

and reward with honor those pastors who did well (1Tim. 5:17). The Greek word for *honor* here implies pay; we probably get our word *honorarium* from the same word.

Both Titus and Timothy demonstrated the use of apostolic authority. It's true we've lost sight of this kind of church structure for the most part. But this shows clearly that in the New Testament the pastors came from an appointment above, not an election below. You may not be able to get back to an apostle/pastor relationship in your present situation, but you may be able to apply some of the principles presented here.

APOSTLES TODAY?
We rarely use the word *apostle* today. We shy away from the term because of *twelve* phobia; we're afraid someone will think we're claiming status with the original twelve! Hey! Those slots are taken. They won't add another foundation to the Holy City and name it after you because of your great tape ministry (Rev. 21:14).

The twelve hold a unique place because they were witnesses of the resurrected Christ (Acts 2:32; 2 Peter 1:16). Never mind for now whether Paul was one of the twelve; he may be one of the two witnesses along with me! Just kidding.

Of course, another unique contribution of the apostles was the New Testament—the Reader's Digest of apostolic teaching!

GENERAL APOSTLES
While the twelve are the special *apostles of the Lamb* (Rev. 21:14), there are other apostles in the New Testament.

Barnabas is named as an apostle in Acts 14:14. Andronicus and Junias are "outstanding among the apostles" (Rom. 16:7). The twelve would not be around to *apostalize* forever. Others would be needed for the next 20 centuries to evangelize and organize whole areas for Christ. Was the gift of the apostle ever removed from the church? Was it ever said to be a temporary gift? Is it possible that some have done the work of an apostle and been called something else?

Some people have evangelized and organized whole areas, and we have called them *missionaries*! This is not to say that all missionaries are apostles; but it's probably true that most apostles are missionaries!

To evangelize an area, a New Testament apostle had gifts of teaching, preaching, and usually miracles (1 Tim. 2:7; 2 Tim. 1:11; 2 Cor. 12:12). Of course by mentioning miracles, Paul may have meant to qualify himself as one of the special apostles. I don't know if the gift of miracles is needed to qualify every general apostle. (Wouldn't hurt to have it!) But the gifts of preaching, teaching, organizing whole areas, and appointing pastors certainly represent apostolic work.

Of course, there will be those who seize the term *apostle* and stick it in their cap as a feather. Some churches are bound to call people *apostles* who couldn't preach their way out of a wet paper bag. Some will buy the title who have neither the gifts, nor calling, nor work of an apostle. But these things will always be.

On the other hand, there are good men doing the work of an apostle who will disdain the title. Historically, a lot of denominations have probably bumped the word *apostle* and inserted the traditional, familiar term *bishop.*

At any rate, we'll be rewarded for our work, not our title. But it's good to distinguish offices and gifts and callings. A title often is a job description!

CHAPTER 13

DEACONS

> Paul and Timothy, servants of Christ Jesus, to all the
> saints at Philippi, together with the overseers and deacons.
> (Phil. 1:1)

Two ministries that should be in every local church are
overseers and *deacons*. *Overseers* is plural here because
Paul is talking about the leaders of a city, not just a local
church; they may or may not be plural in a local church. The
overseers are pastors, a point you can't miss in this book. But
what are deacons? Deacons are servants. The Greek word for
deacon, *diakonos,* means exactly that–servant!

Once again, the New Testament was written in Greek.
And in the Greek mind, words like *janitor, attendant, orderly,*
butler, maid, and *waiter* would have lined up under the word
diakonos: servants. Of course, in that day of bond servants,
slaves, and so on, the term carried a more severe meaning.
Household *diakonoi* were servants (Matt. 22:13) Servants had
no unions, very few rights, and often suffered wrongs. The
servant was at his master's mercy. He was owned by his
master or bound by debt; he was no Wal Mart greeter, who

could walk off the job! There was no servants' court to hear appeals. The servant depended on God for justice.

SERVANTS IN GENERAL

We're all supposed to be servants.

Sitting down, Jesus called the twelve and said, "If anyone wants to be first, he must be the very last, and the servant of all." (Mark 9:35)

Paul called himself a servant (1 Cor.3:5; Eph. 3:7) Even Christ came as a servant:

But made himself nothing, taking the very nature of a servant....(Phil. 2:8a)

For I tell you that Christ has become a servant of the Jews on behalf of God's truth, to confirm the promises made to the Patriarchs. (Rom. 15:9)

For who is greater, the one who is at the table or the one who serves? Is it not the one who is at the table? But I am among you as one who serves. (Luke 22:27)

Middle Eastern hospitality gave the weary visitor a pan of water to wash the road dirt off his feet. But a lowly servant could be given this menial task. Can you believe it? Christ did it!

After that, he poured water into a basin and began to wash his disciples' feet, drying them with the towel that was wrapped around him. (John 13:5)

This lowly servant act freaked Peter out.

He came to Simon Peter, who said to him, "Lord, are you going to wash my feet?

"No," said Peter, "you shall never wash my feet." (John 13:6, 8)

However, Jesus cut Pete no slack:

"Unless I wash you, you have no part with me." (vs. 8b)

Peter was just *two feet* away from dropping off the radar! Being a servant is serious business.

The twelve also did servant work. They held the boat while Christ preached, went for bread, served 4000 and 5000 at different times, and gathered fragments of fish. Good training!

SPECIAL SERVANTS

But while there are servants in general, the local churches needed select servants for specific tasks. These special servants had to be of high character. In fact, Paul set the character bar almost as high for these servants as pastors:

Deacons, likewise, are to be men worthy of respect, sincere, not indulging in much wine, and not pursuing dishonest gain. They must keep hold of the deep truths of the faith with a clear conscience. They must first be tested; and then if there is nothing against them, let them serve as deacons. (1 Tim. 3:8-10)

Your average deacon would flunk the above criteria. If there were a servant Olympics, the only winners would be deacons! Selecting deacons because they're local businessmen or community leaders would have tripped Paul's circuit breakers. (Might as well have a deacon lottery.) Sadly, pew politics plays out in the dishing up of many deacons!

Although these men are servants, they are church officers under the pastor. They have specific responsibilities. They are given authority over their area.

TRANSLATION COMPLICATION

If you're translating the New Testament, how do you distinguish these special servants of the local church from servants in general? The Greek word is the same. Answer: you whittle on the Greek word *diakonos* and carve out a new word–*deacon*.

Now you have two English words for servant: the ordinary word for *servant*, and the special servants of the local church–*deacon*.

If you're talking about servants in general, use the word *servant*. If you're talking about those special high-character servants of the local church, use the word *deacon*. If Bible translators need a word, they sort of...make one up!

WHAT DEACONS DO

Then he rolled up the scroll, gave it back to the attendant and sat down. (Luke 4:20)

The attendant who took the scroll from Jesus was doing the work of a deacon. He was doing synagogue duty. He was a servant of the house. Deacon work is usually physical work. Maintenance, upkeep, and care of God's house is typical deacon work. The Levites who had charge of the tabernacle's upkeep were a tribe of deacons as well as priests.

Joshua was Moses' attendant (Exodus 24:13; 32:17). Elisha apprenticed as Elijah's personal servant (2 Kings 3:11). Deacon work is great training whether you're to be a prophet, a national leader, or a career deacon.

THE MAGNIFICENT SEVEN

In those days when the number of disciples was increasing, the Grecian Jews complained against the Hebraic Jews because their widows were being overlooked in the daily distribution of food.
So the Twelve gathered all the disciples together and said, "It would not be right for us to neglect the ministry of the word of God in order to wait on tables. Brothers, choose seven men from among you who are known to be full of

the Holy Spirit and wisdom. We will turn this responsibility over to them." (Acts 6:1-3)

The overseers/bishops/shepherds/elders/pastors in this situation were the apostles. Their work of ministering the word could easily have been leached away by the legit needs of hungry widows. This work of serving widows was intensive. This wasn't your annual Christmas finger food bash. The needy may have numbered in the hundreds. How easy it is to do good and miss God's best!

What to do? The brothers were asked to choose seven men from among them. Guess what? All seven men chosen were Greek Jews! How could the Greek Jewish widows complain now? (This is God's wisdom.)

The apostles exercised their authority by determining how the seven were chosen and in turning the responsibility over to them. This is a classic example of deacons' work. The men chosen needed to be of high character to ensure fairness.

DEACONS RUNNING THE CHURCH?

Deacons have no authority to govern. They can have authority over an area designated to them. As I said earlier, this authority can be taken back. For deacons to rule the church, though, is like the flight attendants setting the course for the plane or the janitors running city hall. Orderlies don't give orders!

Whoever came up with the idea of deacons running the church is one taco short of a combination plate! Deacons have responsibilities delegated to them by the pastor. Deacons can be removed or reproved by the pastor.

I recently visited a church that I suspect was *owned* by a deacon. I was told he had established the church. He probably was the main contributor to the new building. I'm sure the young pastor had the freedom to do whatever the *deacon* wanted him to do! I wondered if that was why the service was mostly dead; the 40 or so there may have been family. (It's nice to have your own private family church!) True deacons are servants, not owners of churches.

These special servants can be ordained by the pastor or presbytery of the local church, by a regional presbytery, or perhaps by an apostle or regional overseer. Any of the above will work if understood and agreed on by the leadership.

But deacons do not hire or fire pastors! They do not correct pastors. They should never be in a position to withhold a pastor's pay or decide if he will leave or stay.

WOMEN DEACONS

Why not? Why shouldn't a woman be a deacon? Even if you don't believe women should be pastors, you should have no problem with women deacons.

I commend to you our sister Phoebe, a servant of the church of Cenchrea. (Rom. 16:1)

Since Phoebe is mentioned as the *diakonon* of a particular church, she was undoubtedly a deaconess. She's not short on character packing a recommendation from no less than Paul!

There are areas where women could *deac* better than men. Some problems would better lie under a feminine eye. From the nursery (where lots of *changes* are made) to real estate where women realtors may have valuable input (for *land's* sake), the input of women is important.

DEACONS ON THE WAY UP!

In Acts 8, a dynamic evangelist with the gift of miracles takes Samaria by storm. He then evangelizes an African eunuch (vss. 26-39) and sends the gospel *C-mail* (chariot mail) to Ethiopia. That seed is bearing fruit to this day. Who was the awesome evangelist? An ex-deacon, one of the original seven deacons–Philip! He's now Philip the evangelist. Who says you have to stay a deacon forever? Another of the seven deacons achieved honor:

Now Stephen, a man full of God's grace and power, did great wonders and miraculous signs among the people. (Acts 6:8)

Stephen shut down local Jews in debate.

But they couldn't stand up against the wisdom or the Spirit by whom he spoke. (vs. 10)

This deacon's power and wisdom positioned him to be the church's first martyr!

While they were stoning him, Stephen prayed, "Lord Jesus, receive my spirit." (Acts 7:59)

Both Philip and Stephen were launched as deacons and rose to a place in church history. Today's deacons may be tomorrow's evangelists. Or martyrs!

Learning to be a faithful deacon can be basic training for a larger ministry. But let's face it: all deacons aren't going to be kicked up to the level of Benny Hinn! All aren't potential martyrs–and not many volunteer! But just being an ordained deacon is a high honor. How you carry out your calling is more important than what your calling is!

A good deacon is on the job, on time, on his toes, on the alert for the pastor's call, a servant to all, and may get a higher call.

HOW TO RUIN GOOD MEN

A lot of men would have made good deacons, but somebody made them *elders* instead. And ruined them!

To make a master out of a servant before he's mastered being a servant usually ruins him. How many novice Christians are made *elders* and given equal authority with the pastor before they're potty-trained as servants?

Besides, there's no such thing as *lay-elders*, remember! Why keep messing up potentially good deacons? Let the deacons serve under the pastor well. Then let's see if God will take him from being over the parking lot to the pulpit.

But even if he's gifted to be a special servant the rest of his life, the reward is out of this world! Don't make him an elder and rob him of his ministry.

Order Form

To order additional copies, fill out this form and send it along with your check or money order to: Harry Ramey, 305 Dellrose Dr., Mauldin, SC 29662-2225

Cost per copy $9.00 plus $2.00 P&H.

Contact above address for prices on bulk orders.

Ship _____ copies of *Restore the Pastor's Authority* to:

Name_____

Address:_____

City/State/Zip:_____

❑ Check box for signed copy

Please tell us how you found out about this book.

☐ Friend   ☐Internet
☐ Book Store ☐Radio
☐ Newspaper   ☐ Magazine
☐ Other _____